I Follow Instructions.
I LISTEN!

My Amazing Toddler Behavioral Series

An Affirmation-Themed Toddler Book About Listening (Ages 2-4)

By
Suzanne T. Christian

TWORAVENS
BOOKS

Two Little Ravens
CHILDREN'S NON-FICTION BOOKS

Paperback Edition: 9781964202389
Hardcover Edition: 9781964202396
Digital Edition: 9781964202402

Published in the United States by Two Ravens Books LLC,
254 Chapman Rd, Ste 209, Newark DE 19702

'Expand the mind, free the imagination, one title at a time.'
www.tworavensbooks.com

Welcome to
"I Follow Instructions.
I Listen!"

This playful picture book is a delightful collection of easy-to-follow affirmations for young children. As you explore its pages, your child will discover how focusing, paying attention, and following directions build confidence and positive behavior.

Each page features vibrant illustrations and relatable scenarios, encouraging your toddler to pause, listen, and learn. By making this book a regular part of your reading routine, you can watch your child's listening skills blossom, knowing repetition is one of the best ways to teach.

Get ready for a journey of mindful listening, cooperation, and plenty of fun with your toddler!

Suzanne T. Christian

Listening helps me
Learn new things!

When Mommy calls my name, I stop and look. I listen!

I keep my ears wide open like a bunny.

Daddy says, **"Come here,"** and I go right away.

I use my "listening ears" to hear every word.

I wait my turn to talk. I listen!

The teacher says,
"Please sit,"
so I sit like a happy
hedgehog.

Listening is my superpower!

When someone is talking to me,
I look and listen!

"The big elephant ears game",
helps me pay attention!

I say, "Okay!" when my teacher gives me directions.

I see your face, I hear
your words!

At story time,
I open my ears
and my eyes.
I listen!

Wiggle, wiggle—
now I'm all ears!

When I hear **'Time to eat,'** I walk to my seat!

I follow steps like "Pick up toys" and "Wash hands".

When I hear **"Stop"**,
I freeze like a statue.

When I listen, I stay safe!

When I hear **"Bedtime,"** I get ready for bed.

I say **"yes!"** when I understand.

Listening makes me a great helper. **I listen!**

I Follow Instructions. I Listen!

The End!

My Amazing Toddler Behavioral Series

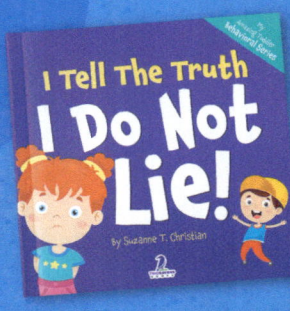

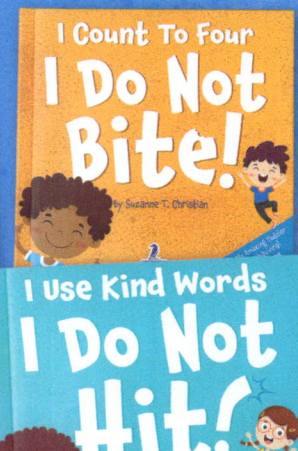

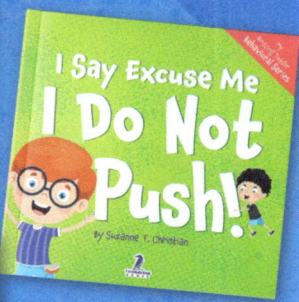

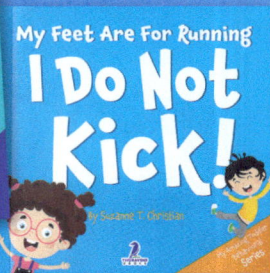

Check Out
Suzanne T. Christian's beloved series
'My Amazing Toddler Behavioral Series'.
Young readers are sure to enjoy!

Dear Amazing Reader,

Thank you for diving into **I Follow Instructions. I Listen!** with me. If this book touched your heart or made a difference for a young reader, I'd be grateful if you could share your thoughts in a review. Your feedback inspires my future work and helps others discover the magic within these pages.

I'd love to hear from you directly if you have suggestions or ideas for improving the book. Please feel free to reach out to me at **suzanne.christian@tworavensbooks.com.** Your voice counts, and I cherish it deeply.

With heartfelt gratitude,